MW01680354

short talks for kids

Ages 4-7

Britney Rule & Linda Prince

LEATHERWOOD PRESS

Leatherwood Press books are available exclusively
through Deseret Book Distributors.

For details, write or telephone
Deseret Book Distributors, 57 West South Temple
Salt Lake City, Utah 84101
(801) 534-1515

Leatherwood Press LLC
8160 South Highland Drive
Sandy, Utah 84093
www.leatherwoodpress.com

ISBN: 978-1-59992-080-1

Printed in the United States.

○ ● Contents ● ○

○ ● Chapter 1 ● ○

Baptism and Confirmation

I Can Be Baptized and Confirmed

I will be baptized when I am eight years old.

I will do this to show my love for Heavenly Father.

I will do this to obey His commandments and to get on the right path to return to Him.

After I am baptized, I will be confirmed a member of the Church.

Then I will receive the gift of the Holy Ghost.

The Holy Ghost will guide and protect me throughout my life.

I will show my faith in Jesus Christ by being baptized and confirmed.

Visual Aid: GAPK 601—Baptism

I Can Be Baptized When I Turn Eight

When I turn eight years old, I will get baptized.

My dad or another priesthood holder will baptize me.

All my sins will be washed away.

Then I will be confirmed a member of the Church.

I will receive the gift of the Holy Ghost.

The Holy Ghost will help me make good choices.

I am excited to turn eight so I can be baptized and receive the Holy Ghost.

Visual Aid: GAPK 602—The Gift of the Holy Ghost

Taking the Sacrament Renews My Baptismal Covenants

Taking the sacrament is like getting baptized again.

When I take the sacrament, I make promises to Heavenly Father.

I promise that I will keep the commandments and that I will always remember Jesus Christ.

I promise that I will try to be like Jesus.

I will make the same promises when I am baptized.

I will promise to keep the commandments and always remember Jesus.

I am thankful I can take the sacrament each week.

Visual Aid: GAPK 604—Passing the Sacrament

○ ● Chapter 2 ● ○

Family

Heavenly Father Gave Me a Family and I Can Strengthen My Family Now

Heavenly Father planned for me to come to a family.

He knew that my family would help me learn and grow.

He also knew that I could strengthen them.

I can do this by being kind to all the members of my family.

I can do this by having faith.

I can do this by setting an example for my family by doing what is right.

I am grateful that Heavenly Father sent me to my family.

Visual Aid: GAPK 616—Family Togetherness

Families in the Scriptures Teach Me How I Can Strengthen My Family

Families in the scriptures teach me how I can strengthen my family.

Nephi helped his family.

Nephi helped his brothers understand what their father taught them.

I can teach my family the gospel too.

Nephi had faith that the Lord could help him build a ship.

Nephi showed his brothers how to have faith in the Lord.

My faith can help my family have faith.

I can help my family just like Nephi.

Visual Aid: GAPK 617—Search the Scriptures

The Scriptures Teach Me about Families

Families in the scriptures teach me how to make my family stronger.

Nephi helped his brothers.

Alma taught his sons.

The stripling warriors were blessed by their mothers.

I can help my family too.

I can help them choose the right.

I am thankful for my family.

Visual Aid: GAPK 303—Nephi Subdues His Rebellious Brothers

Each Member of My Family Has a Divine Role

My family is very special to me.

I have a father that takes care of me.

I have a mother that hugs me when I feel sad.

I have brothers and sisters that play with me.

I have grandparents that love me.

I have aunts and uncles that tell me stories.

I am thankful for my family.

(Change wording according to child's family situation.)

Visual Aid: GAPK 616—Family Togetherness

Heavenly Father Gave My Family the Gospel

Heavenly Father wants my family to be strong.

He gave us scriptures to teach us the gospel.

I can read the scriptures with my family every day.

Heavenly Father asks us to pray to Him.

My family will be stronger if we pray together every day.

The prophets teach us to have family home evening.

My family will be blessed if we have family home evening each week.

I am glad Heavenly Father gave my family the gospel.

Visual Aid: GAPK 606—Family Prayer

The Priesthood Can Bless and Strengthen My Family

The priesthood can bless my family.

If I am sick, I can get a priesthood blessing to help me feel better.

If I am scared, a priesthood blessing can help me feel peace.

And if I need special help, I can get a priesthood blessing to help me.

I am glad that Heavenly Father gave us the priesthood.

Visual Aid: GAPK 613—Administering to the Sick

Priesthood Blessings Help Me

Many of the early Saints in Nauvoo were bitten by mosquitoes that made them very sick.

Joseph Smith gave the people priesthood blessings.

He blessed all the people who were sick.

The people were all healed.

I can also get a priesthood blessing when I am sick to help me get well.

I can get a blessing when I am scared or lonely so I can feel better.

A priesthood blessing can bless me when I need special help.

I am thankful the priesthood blesses me.

Visual Aid: GAPK 401—The Prophet Joseph Smith

Chapter 3

Following the Holy Ghost

The Holy Ghost Will Help Me Live Righteously

The Holy Ghost will help me make good choices.

The Holy Ghost will speak with a still small voice.

The Holy Ghost will warn me of danger.

The Holy Ghost will help me know when I need to repent.

I am thankful for the gift of the Holy Ghost.

Visual Aid: GAPK 602—The Gift of the Holy Ghost

I Will Receive the Holy Ghost after I Am Baptized

When I am eight, I will receive the gift of the Holy Ghost.

The Holy Ghost can bless me in many ways.

The Holy Ghost will speak to me in my heart and my mind.

The Holy Ghost will prompt me to repent.

The Holy Ghost will help me to always live righteously.

I can have the Holy Ghost with me all the time after I am confirmed.

Visual Aid: GAPK 602—The Gift of the Holy Ghost

○ ● Chapter 4 ● ○

Forgiveness

The Prophet Teaches Me that I Should Love and Forgive Others

When someone does something mean to me, I have two choices.

I can get mad and grumpy and act mean back.

Or I can forgive the other person.

To forgive means to be nice even if the other person isn't.

To forgive means to not be angry at others.

To forgive means to love others.

The prophet teaches us that we should forgive people.

I will follow the prophet's teachings and forgive others.

Visual Aid: GAPK 520—Gordon B. Hinckley

Jesus Taught Me How to Forgive

When Jesus was hanging on the cross, He forgave the soldiers.

He wasn't angry at them for following orders.

He knew they didn't know they were doing something wrong.

He asked Heavenly Father to forgive them too.

The prophet teaches us to be like Jesus.

The prophet teaches us to forgive.

I can forgive others like Jesus did.

Visual Aid: GAPK 230—The Crucifixion

○ ● Chapter 5 ● ○

Heavenly Father's Plan

I Accepted Heavenly Father's Plan and I Have a Divine Destiny

In the premortal world, I learned of Heavenly Father's plan for me.

It is called the plan of salvation.

I accepted this plan because I knew it would make me happy.

Heavenly Father wants me to learn and grow and be tested.

He wants me to do this so I can be like Him someday.

I want to become like Heavenly Father, so I will follow His plan.

Visual Aid: GAPK 607—Young Girl Speaking at Church

Heavenly Father Gave Me Agency

When I lived with Heavenly Father,

He gave me a very special gift.

This gift is called agency.

Agency is being able to make my own choices.

Heavenly Father hoped I would choose His plan for me.

Satan wanted me to choose another plan.

I decided to follow Heavenly Father's plan.

I know Heavenly Father's plan will make me happy.

Visual Aid: GAPK 605—Young Boy Praying

Jesus Created the World for All of God's Children

As part of Heavenly Father's plan, Jesus created the earth.

He did this for all of Heavenly Father's children.

Adam and Eve were the first people on the earth.

They were our first parents.

They made choices that allowed us to come to earth.

I am grateful to Adam and Eve.

I am grateful that Jesus created this world for me.

Visual Aid: GAPK 101—Adam and Eve

○ ● Chapter 6 ● ○

I Am a Child of God

I Am a Child of God and I Am Created in His Image

I am a child of God, who loves me.

I lived with Him in the premortal world.

He created me in His image.

That means I look like Him!

I will keep all the commandments.

I will do what my parents ask me to do.

I will be kind to all of Heavenly Father's children.

Then I can live with Heavenly Father and Jesus someday.

Visual Aid: GAPK 616—Family Togetherness

Because I Am His child, I Will Serve God

I know that I am a child of God.

He loves me very much.

He has asked me to serve Him.

I will do this by having faith.

I will do this by keeping the commandments.

I will do this by helping others.

I will do this by sharing my testimony.

Because I am Heavenly Father's child,

I will serve him with all my heart, might, mind, and strength.

Visual Aid: GAPK 605—Young Boy Praying

● ○ ● ○ ●

I Am Thankful to Be a Beloved Child of God

I am thankful that I am a child of God.

I know that Heavenly Father loves me.

He has blessed me with a body that works.

He has blessed me with a loving family.

He has blessed me with the gospel.

He has blessed me with prayer.

He has blessed me with the scriptures and prophets.

I am glad I am a child of God and that He loves me.

Visual Aid: GAPK 606—Family Prayer

I Am Thankful for My Body and I Know My Body Is a Temple

Jesus Christ says that my body is a temple.

The Holy Ghost can dwell in me.

So I will keep my body clean and pure.

I will not get tattoos.

I will dress modestly.

I will only eat healthy foods.

I will exercise so my body will be strong.

I am thankful for my body.

I know my body is a temple.

Visual Aid: GAPK 617—Search the Scriptures

Heavenly Father Loves All of His Children

After Jesus died, He was resurrected.

Then He appeared to many people in the Holy Land.

When Jesus left, He went to bless the Nephites.

Heavenly Father loves all of His children.

So He sent Jesus Christ to be our Savior.

I am glad that I am Heavenly Father's child and that He loves me.

Visual Aid: GAPK 608—Christ and Children from around the World

○ ● Chapter 7 ● ○

Jesus Christ, Our Savior

Jesus Christ Is My Savior

I know that Jesus Christ is my Savior.

He did some very important things for me.

Jesus knew I would do many things wrong.

He felt pain for my sins.

So I can be forgiven if I repent.

Jesus died and was resurrected.

He did this so that after I die I can live again.

Jesus did these things for me because He loves me.

I love Him and know that He is my Savior.

Visual Aid: GAPK 239—The Resurrected Jesus Christ

Jesus Died for Us So We Can Return to Heavenly Father

Jesus is the Savior of all mankind.

He saved us from our sins. He saved us from death.

He did this by suffering for us in the Garden of Gethsemane.

He did this by dying for us on the cross.

He did this by being resurrected.

We can live forever and be happy.

All we must do is repent and do what is right.

Jesus is my Savior, and I love Him.

Visual Aid: GAPK 230—The Crucifixion

Jesus Christ Showed Me How to Do the Will of Heavenly Father

Jesus Christ showed me how to do the will of Heavenly Father.

Jesus was born on earth and grew up.

Jesus obeyed all of Heavenly Father's commandments.

Jesus did everything Heavenly Father asked Him to do.

Jesus asks me to follow Him.

I will follow Jesus by always trying to do Heavenly Father's will.

Visual Aid: GAPK 208—John the Baptist Baptizing Jesus

Jesus Christ Will Come to Earth Again

Jesus came to earth as a little baby a long time ago.

He was a little child, just like me.

Then He died and was resurrected.

He would never die again.

One day, Jesus will come back to earth.

Everybody will know that He has come.

It will be a happy day for the good people.

I am glad that Jesus will come back to earth someday.

Visual Aid: GAPK 238—The Second Coming

Prophets Have Always Taught about Jesus Christ

Prophets knew about Jesus long before He came to earth.

Heavenly Father told them Jesus would come.

Prophets spoke about Jesus Christ in the scriptures.

They told us where He would be born.

They told us how He would help all people.

They knew He would die for us.

I am happy that the prophets tell me about Jesus Christ.

Visual Aid: GAPK 113—Isaiah Writes of Christ's Birth

Jesus Came to Earth Like the Prophets Prophesied

Jesus Christ was born. A bright new star shone in the sky.

The star was above the stable where Jesus was born.

Shepherds came to see the baby Jesus.

Wise men from far away followed the new star.

They found Jesus and gave Him gifts.

The prophets' words were right. Jesus was born.

Visual Aid: GAPK 202—Announcement of Christ's Birth to the Shepherds

I Love My Savior, Jesus Christ, and His Restored Gospel

I love Jesus Christ and His restored gospel.

I love Him because He is my Savior.

I love His restored gospel because it is true.

Living the gospel makes me happy.

I want to show Jesus that I love Him.

So I will obey His commandments and do what is right.

I love my Savior, Jesus Christ, and His restored gospel.

Visual Aid: GAPK 227—Jesus Praying in Gethsemane

○ ● Chapter 8 ● ○

Joseph Smith and the Restored Gospel

Jesus Restored His Gospel through the Prophet Joseph Smith

Jesus Christ taught true gospel.

After Jesus left, people stopped believing in the gospel.

So Heavenly Father took it away.

Jesus restored the gospel through Joseph Smith.

The gospel teaches us how to be happy and how to treat others.

I love the Savior and His restored gospel.

Visual Aid: GAPK 401—The Prophet Joseph Smith

Joseph Smith's First Vision

Joseph Smith didn't know which church to join.

He prayed to Heavenly Father to ask.

Heavenly Father and Jesus Christ appeared.

They told him that all of the churches were wrong.

Joseph Smith listened to Jesus and Heavenly Father. Joseph became a prophet of God.

Joseph Smith restored the true Church.

I am grateful to Joseph Smith.

Visual Aid: GAPK 403—The First Vision

I Am Grateful for the Restored Gospel in My Life

I am blessed to have the restored gospel in my life.

The gospel has helped me learn many things.

Because of the restored gospel, I know I am a child of God.

I know that Jesus Christ lives.

I know that the Book of Mormon is true.

I am thankful to be a member of this Church.

I am grateful to have the restored gospel in my life.

Visual Aid: GAPK 406—Joseph Smith Receives the Gold Plates

Chapter 9

Missionary Work

I Will Share the Gospel with Others Because I Know Heavenly Father Loves Them

I know that we are all children of God.

I know that Heavenly Father loves us all.

Some of my friends don’t know about Heavenly Father.

So I will tell my friends about Him.

I will tell them about Jesus.

I will tell them about the commandments.

I will tell them I know the Church is true.

I will share the gospel with others.

Visual Aid: GAPK 612—Missionaries Teach the Gospel of Jesus Christ

I Will Prepare to Be a Missionary by Being Faithful and Obedient

I can prepare to be a missionary now.

Missionaries teach people about the scriptures.

I can prepare for a mission by reading the scriptures every day.

Missionaries teach people to pray.

Missionaries are friendly to people even if they are different.

I can prepare for a mission by being friendly to everyone.

I can prepare for a mission now by having faith and obeying the commandments.

Visual Aid: GAPK 605—Young Boy Praying

I Can Prepare to Be a Missionary Now

I can prepare to be a missionary now.

I will choose the right.

I will obey Heavenly Father and my parents.

I will listen to the prophet.

I will be nice to my family.

I am excited to be a missionary someday.

Visual Aid: GAPK 612—Missionaries Teach the Gospel of Jesus Christ

Living the Gospel Standards Helps Me Be a Missionary Now

When I choose the right, people notice me.

When I am nice to my brother or sister, I help others remember to be nice.

When I choose not to drink or smoke or say bad words, I teach other people not to do these bad things.

When I live the gospel standards, I teach other people about the gospel.

That is what Jesus did.

He was a good example to those around Him.

I can be a missionary now by choosing the right.

Visual Aid: GAPK 615—Serving One Another

I Bless My Friends When I Tell Them about the Gospel

Some of my friends are not members of our Church.

They don't know all the wonderful things I know.

I want all my friends to be happy,

So I tell them about the gospel.

It's fun to share my testimony.

It's fun to talk about Jesus Christ and what He taught us.

I bless my friends when I tell them about the gospel.

Visual Aid: GAPK 607—Young Girl Speaking at Church

○ ● Chapter 10 ● ○

Prayer

I Can Pray to Heavenly Father to Thank Him for My Blessings and Ask for Help

Heavenly Father wants me to pray to Him.

When I pray, I thank Him for all His blessings.

I ask Him to bless my family and friends.

I ask Him to bless the prophet.

I ask Him to bless all the people in the world.

And I ask Him to bless me to do what is right.

I also ask Him any questions that I have.

Heavenly Father will hear and answer my prayers.

Visual Aid: GAPK 605—Young Boy Praying

Heavenly Father Will Always Listen to and Answer My Prayers

I love to pray to Heavenly Father.

I can pray with my family or by myself.

I can pray anytime during the day or night.

Heavenly Father will hear me no matter where I am when I pray.

He will answer my prayers.

Sometimes the answer will be no.

Sometimes it will be yes.

I am glad to know that Heavenly Father always answers my prayers.

Visual Aid: GAPK 605—Young Boy Praying

I Learn about Prayer from the Scriptures

When I say a prayer, I start out by saying, "Dear Heavenly Father."

Then I thank Him for my blessings.

And ask Him for things that I need.

I end the prayer in the name of Jesus Christ.

And then I say, "Amen."

I am glad I can pray to Heavenly Father.

Visual Aid: GAPK 605—Young Boy Praying

I Can Learn about Prayer from Jesus Christ in the Scriptures

When Jesus was on the earth, He taught His disciples to pray.

He told them to start the prayer by addressing Heavenly Father.

He said they should say thanks for their blessings, then ask for the things they needed.

Jesus said they should pray in His name.

So I should say my prayers the same way.

I can learn how to pray by reading the scriptures.

Visual Aid: GAPK 617—Search the Scriptures

I Can Pray Anytime, Anywhere

Alma's people were captured by wicked people.

The wicked people told them not to pray.

Alma's people needed Heavenly Father's help.

They prayed in their hearts instead of out loud.

This way the guards couldn't hear them.

But Heavenly Father could still hear them.

He answered their prayers and helped them.

I can pray to Heavenly Father anytime, anywhere.

Heavenly Father always hears my prayers.

Visual Aid: GAPK 606—Family Prayer

Heavenly Father Knows Me and Will Answer My Prayers in Ways that Are Best for Me

Sometimes I need Heavenly Father's help or an answer.

I can ask Him for it when I pray.

Heavenly Father loves me and wants to bless me.

He wants to give me what is best for me.

Sometimes that means His answer is "yes."

Sometimes His answer is "no" or "later."

I am thankful that Heavenly Father answers my prayers.

Visual Aid: GAPK 605—Young Boy Praying

Heavenly Father Answers My Prayers through the Holy Ghost, the Scriptures, and Others

Heavenly Father answers my prayers.

Sometimes He answers them through the Holy Ghost.

Sometimes Heavenly Father answers my prayers through the scriptures.

Heavenly Father also answers my prayers through others.

I am glad that Heavenly Father always answers my prayers.

Visual Aid: GAPK 605—Young Boy Praying

Chapter 11

Prophets

I Will Follow the Prophet

The President of the Church is our prophet.

He teaches us about the commandments.

He warns of us things that are bad for us.

When the prophet speaks by the Holy Ghost, it is as if Heavenly Father were speaking.

I know that the prophet speaks the truth.

I know that I can be happy by doing what he says.

I will follow the prophet.

Visual Aid: GAPK 520—Gordon B. Hinckley

The Prophet Holds Priesthood Keys

Our prophet holds priesthood keys from God.

These keys give the prophet power to run the Church.

These keys help us do missionary and temple work.

Jesus Christ directs the Church through the prophet with these keys.

The prophet teaches us what Heavenly Father and Jesus want us to hear.

I am grateful that our prophet has God's power to direct the Church.

Visual Aid: GAPK 520—Gordon B. Hinckley

The Prophet Teaches Us to Read the Scriptures

President Hinckley asked everyone to read the Book of Mormon.

He said we would be blessed if we read it.

I can read the Book of Mormon every day.

I can pray about the Book of Mormon.

The Holy Ghost will tell me it is true.

I will be blessed when I read the Book of Mormon.

I can follow the prophet's teachings.

Visual Aid: GAPK 617—Search the Scriptures

The Prophet Teaches Me What I Must Do to Live with God Again

The prophet teaches us how to return to Heavenly Father someday.

The prophet teaches us to be kind to others.

He teaches us to pay our tithing.

He teaches us to obey the commandments.

He teaches us we must be baptized.

He teaches us we must be married in the temple.

Then we can return to live with Heavenly Father someday.

I am glad Heavenly Father gave us a prophet.

Visual Aid: GAPK 520—Gordon B. Hinckley

The Prophets and Apostles Teach Me How to Serve

The prophets and apostles teach me about service.

Our prophet does many things to serve us.

He travels around the world to teach people the gospel.

The prophet spends all of his time serving us.

He does this because he loves us.

I am glad for prophets and apostles who teach me how to serve.

Visual Aid: GAPK 520—Gordon B. Hinckley

○ ● Chapter 12 ● ○

Repentance

Heavenly Father Forgives All Who Truly Repent

When I do something wrong, Heavenly Father is sad.

He wants me to repent when I make a bad choice.

So I will say I am sorry for the bad thing I have done.

I will fix my mistake if I can.

Heavenly Father will forgive me if I repent.

He loves me and wants me to choose the right.

Visual Aid: GAPK 605—Young Boy Praying

I Can Learn about Repentance from the Scriptures

The Book of Mormon tells about a man named Enos.

One day Enos was hunting in the woods.

He wanted to pray to Heavenly Father to repent of his sins.

He prayed all day and into the night.

He heard a voice from heaven saying that his sins were forgiven.

Enos was very happy.

I can also repent when I make mistakes.

If I repent, Heavenly Father will forgive me too.

Visual Aid: GAPK 305—Enos Praying

The Atonement of Jesus Christ Makes it Possible for Me to Repent

Jesus Christ knew that I would sin. Then I could not live with Heavenly Father again.

So Jesus suffered for my sins.

This is called the atonement.

Because of the atonement, I can be forgiven if I repent.

I will remember what Jesus did for me.

I will try not to sin.

When I do sin, I will repent.

Then I can return to live with Heavenly Father and Jesus someday.

Visual Aid: GAPK 227—Jesus Praying in Gethsemane

○ ● Chapter 13 ● ○

Sabbath Day

I Will Keep the Sabbath Day Holy

Heavenly Father wants me to keep the Sabbath day holy.

On Sunday, I will do things that help me feel close to Jesus.

I will go to church.

I will visit people who are sick.

I will read the scriptures.

I will choose to do things on the Sabbath that will make Heavenly Father happy.

Visual Aid: GAPK 604—Passing the Sacrament

The Sabbath is the Day We Honor Heavenly Father

Heavenly Father wants us to keep the Sabbath day holy.

Jesus taught about the Sabbath when he gave the commandments to Moses a long time ago.

He wanted the children of Israel to have one special day when they honored God.

I will keep the Sabbath day holy.

I will go to church each week.

I will sing and listen in Primary.

I will read stories about Jesus Christ.

I will spend time with my family.

The Sabbath is the day we honor Heavenly Father.

Visual Aid: GAPK 617—Search the Scriptures

Chapter 14

Service

I Can Serve Heavenly Father by Serving Others

When King Benjamin was old he gave a speech to his people.

He reminded them that he had tried to serve them.

He said that when he served his people, he was also serving God.

He taught his people that they could serve God by serving others too.

King Benjamin is a good example of service.

When I serve my friends or my family, I am also serving Heavenly Father.

Visual Aid: GAPK 615—Serving One Another

Many People Serve Me

When people do nice things for me, I want to serve them.

My parents serve me by taking care of me.

My friends serve me by being kind to me.

My teachers serve me by helping me learn.

My Church leaders serve me by teaching me what is right.

When other people serve me, I'm happy so I want to serve too.

Visual Aid: GAPK 615—Serving One Another

Because Others Serve Me, I Too Want to Serve

When other people serve me, it makes me feel good inside.

When they serve me, I know that they love me.

This makes me so happy that I want to serve other people too!

I can help my mother when she is getting dinner ready.

I can give my friends a hug if they are feeling sad.

I can do my chores without being asked.

I can be a peacemaker in my family.

I want to serve others when they serve me.

Visual Aid: GAPK 615—Serving One Another

I Can Show Respect and Kindness to All of God's Children

Heavenly Father loves all His children, no matter who they are.

I want to show Heavenly Father I love Him.

So I will show respect and kindness to everyone.

I will be friendly and say hello to everyone.

When someone needs help, I will lend a hand.

When I notice that someone feels bad, I will try to cheer them up.

I will try to be kind even when someone isn't kind to me.

I will show Heavenly Father that I love all His children too.

Visual Aid: GAPK 616—Family Togetherness

○ ● Chapter 15 ● ○

Scriptures

The Scriptures Teach Me the Gospel

I love to read the scriptures.

They teach me about Heavenly Father.

They teach me about Jesus Christ.

The scriptures teach me how I can return to live with Heavenly Father and Jesus.

I want to live with Them someday, so I will do what the scriptures say.

I will keep the commandments and listen to the Holy Ghost.

I will love my family and obey my parents.

I will do what the scriptures teach me to do.

Visual Aid: GAPK 617—Search the Scriptures

The Bible and the Book of Mormon Testify of Jesus Christ

Jesus loves me, and He is my Savior.

He came to earth to show us the way.

The Bible testifies of Jesus.

The Book of Mormon also testifies of Jesus.

I will read the Bible and Book of Mormon.

I want to learn about Jesus.

I want to follow Him.

Visual Aid: GAPK 326—The Bible and Book of Mormon: Two Witnesses

Bible Stories Teach Me How to Live the Gospel

Bible stories teach me how to live the gospel.

From Daniel, I learn that Heavenly Father will protect me.

From Moses, I learn the Lord can do miracles.

From Esther, I learn that the Lord watches over His people.

From Peter, I learn to have faith in Jesus.

From Jesus, I learn to trust in Heavenly Father.

I will read the Bible so I can learn how to live the gospel.

Visual Aid: GAPK 212—Sermon on the Mount

The Book of Mormon Teaches Me How to Live the Gospel

When I read the Book of Mormon,

I learn how to live the gospel.

Nephi shows me how to obey the Lord.

Mosiah teaches me that I should serve others.

Alma teaches me about missionary work.

Ether teaches me to have faith like the brother of Jared.

Moroni teaches me to ask the Lord for help.

Book of Mormon stories teach me that I will be happy if I keep the commandments.

I love to read the Book of Mormon.

Visual Aid: GAPK 325—The Gold Plates

The Doctrine and Covenants Teaches Me How to Live the Gospel

The Doctrine and Covenants is a book of revelations.

In this book, Jesus teaches us about the gospel.

He tells us how to organize His Church.

He tells us how to baptize and bless the sacrament.

He tells us to always love and serve others.

He tells us how to be eternal families.

I will follow the teachings in the Doctrine and Covenants.

Visual Aid: GAPK 402—Joseph Smith Seeks Wisdom in the Bible

○ ● Chapter 16 ● ○

Temples

I Can Receive Special Blessings in the Temple

The temple is a beautiful place.

When I am older, I will go to the temple.

I will receive special blessings and make promises.

After I go to the temple for myself, I will go for people who have died.

I will help them receive their temple blessings.

Someday I will be married in the temple.

The temple is a blessing for my family and me.

Visual Aid: GAPK 502—Salt Lake Temple

My Tithing Helps to Build Temples

Heavenly Father gives me everything I have.

All He asks is that I give one-tenth of my money back to Him.

When I earn money, I put one-tenth of it in an envelope.

Then I give the envelope to my bishop.

The Church uses tithing money for many important things.

One of these things is building temples.

When I see the temple, I can know that my tithing money helped build it.

Visual Aid: GAPK 505—Washington D.C. Temple

The Early Saints Built Temples

The early Saints were poor.

Sometimes they did not have much food to eat or warm shoes and clothes to wear.

But they knew that temples were very important.

They worked one day out of ten to help build the temple instead of working in their fields.

They worked hard to make beautiful temples.

I am grateful that we have temples today.

Visual Aid: GAPK 500—Kirtland Temple

I Will Do Family History Work So My Ancestors Can Receive Temple Blessings

I am blessed to have the gospel in my life.

Some of my ancestors didn't know about the Church.

After they died, they were taught the gospel.

But they can't be baptized and confirmed without my help.

They can't receive their temple ordinances without my help.

When I get older, I can help my ancestors receive their temple blessings.

Then they can live with Heavenly Father again.

Visual Aid: GAPK 504—Temple Baptismal Font

I Will Be Reverent, Dress Modestly, and Speak Kindly to Be Worthy to Enter the Temple

I can prepare now to go to the temple someday.

In the temple, people are very reverent because it is a special place.

I can prepare to go to the temple by being reverent in church.

In the temple, we promise to dress modestly.

I can prepare to go to the temple by being modest now.

In the temple, people speak kindly and quietly.

I can prepare to go to the temple by speaking kindly to people I meet.

I am glad I can go to the temple when I am older.

Visual Aid: GAPK 617—Search the Scriptures